Call of th

For Tony, my selkie son

Contents

Chapter 1

"Go away," said Ryan. He stood on the shore, arms folded, his body a barrier between the headland behind him and the girl in front of him.

"Why can't I go with you?" Cilla sounded hurt and puzzled.

"I want to be by myself," said Ryan.

"What's the problem?"

"I just need a little time to think," said Ryan. "On my own."

Cilla tossed her head and her hair lifted in the breeze. "Suit yourself," she said and turned away.

Ryan sighed with relief and began climbing the rocks. He and Cilla had been friends since her family came to the beach town two years ago. Cilla's family had moved into the house just across the road. Ryan had been glad to have someone his own age in the small community of mostly retired people. He hated sending Cilla away, but he couldn't risk her seeing what was at the bay. She was hopeless at keeping secrets.

He pulled himself up the jagged rocks. Skinned knuckles and shins had taught him which handholds and rocks to trust with his weight. He made his way over the headland towards the hidden access he had discovered a few months ago.

Ryan glanced back to make sure Cilla wasn't following him, then he leapt off the rocks onto a small half-circle of sand wedged between the headland and a cliff face. It looked as though he could go no further.

He turned to a large boulder jutting out from the sheer cliff, which seemed welded into the cliff face itself. He scaled the rock and slid over the top. A gap between the side of the boulder and the cliff led to a narrow tunnel.

Dropping to his knees, Ryan wriggled through the opening. It took several seconds for his eyes to become accustomed to the dark cavern, then he moved ahead. Around a bend in the tunnel, a glimmer of light lit up his path.

As he scrambled towards the exit, he thought of the day in early summer when he had fled to the sanctuary of the bay. Sheltered from the fierce coastal winds, the bay was a haven from the many storms at home.

Ryan didn't know exactly what had made his parents start quarrelling, but the angry words and slammed doors made him feel sick to his stomach. He would shut himself in his room, turn up the volume on his stereo, and play his harmonica to block out the raised voices. But the animosity filling the house still suffocated him.

One day, when he heard his parents start to quarrel again, he left the house and made his way to the bay. After emerging from the tunnel, he was buffeted by wind squalls as he slid down the steep bank towards the rocks. Spray from the ocean mingled with the tears on his face.

A bellow from beyond the rocky point startled him. It started as a deep roar and ended with a harsh bark like a dog being strangled. The bellow rang out again. It must be a large animal to make that much noise, Ryan thought.

Ryan clambered around the point and stopped. On the far side of the bay, a female fur seal lay in the shelter of some rocks. Her body shuddered and swayed as she raised her head, swinging it from side to side.

Unwilling to provoke or disturb the creature, Ryan crouched beside a large boulder. He watched as the seal heaved herself upright and supported her body weight on her front flippers. She seemed to be in distress.

She flapped and whacked her splayed hind flippers on a flat rock. Ripples spread down the sleek length of her body. Her huge dark eyes bulged and spiky whiskers drooped from beneath her nose.

Ryan squinted as a dark, shiny lump slid from underneath the seal. The animal groaned and hitched itself forward, shedding more of the glistening mass. The steaming bundle flopped onto the rock, lay still for a moment, then twitched.

The seal gave a hoarse cry, turned her head towards the object and began licking away the glossy covering. Ryan watched in amazement as the bundle moved and raised a small head. It was a baby seal, a pup.

The pup lay there for a moment, its head turning from side to side in bewilderment. Then, guided by instinct, it moved awkwardly on its flippers to the shadowy bulk of its mother. The pup pushed and nuzzled its snout into its mother's side, and milk began trickling from the corners of the pup's mouth.

The mother seal spread out in a comfortable position, laid her head down and dozed. Ryan smiled as a snore like an old man's came from the animal.

Ryan watched the mother and her baby for a long time. The sun was low in the sky when he retraced his steps around the point and climbed the bank to the opening in the cliff leading towards home. He had a warm feeling inside when he thought of the birth he had just witnessed.

He wanted to share the news with Cilla, but she would be unable to resist telling other people. The mother seal and her pup needed privacy. There was only one person he could trust.

The following Saturday morning, after his father had gone to the office "just to catch up", Ryan worked with his mother in the family's overgrown garden. Still angry from a sharp exchange with Ryan's father, she slammed a spade into the compacted ground, loosening the soil around clumps of weeds, then grasped them at their base and ripped them out. Ryan and his mother worked together in silence, with only an occasional grunt as one of them did battle with a particularly stubborn weed.

Now and then, Ryan glanced at his mother, noticing the tight line of her lips soften as the physical effort and the smell of freshly turned soil eased her tension. After a time she straightened and wiped the back of her hand across her forehead, streaking her skin with mud.

"Why don't we go for a swim?" Ryan asked.

"Now, that's a very good idea," she said, smiling at him.

"I'll take you somewhere special," he said.

They made their way over the headland. "This way," said Ryan, scrambling up the boulder next to the cliff face.

"I didn't know this was here," his mother said as they wriggled through the tunnel.

They slid down the far side of the cliff and were picking their way over rocks towards the point when Ryan touched his mother's arm.

"Follow me quietly, Mum," he said. "I want to show you something."

They rounded the point and Ryan scanned the bay. Nothing disturbed the curve of secluded sand. Disappointment rose in his throat.

Then he saw them. The mother seal lay nestled among low rocks on the far side of the bay, suckling her pup.

"Look," he said, pointing towards the seals. "Over there."

"They're beautiful," she exclaimed.

They watched the seals in silence. Sun slanted across the rocks and the mother seal stretched out to absorb its warmth.

"The mother's coat is such a wonderful rich chestnut," his mother said. "It shines like copper."

"Copper," said Ryan. "That can be her name."

"It's unusual for a seal to give birth away from a rookery," his mother observed. "She must have gone into labour on her way to join other seals."

Ryan and his mother moved on to the sandy bay. The mother seal raised herself on her flippers, tossed her head and snorted a warning. The pup fixed huge, solemn eyes on the intruders as though it was assessing them.

"Let's go for our swim," said his mother. "Maybe Copper will think I'm just another seal with her pup."

"I'm a teenager," Ryan protested. "You can't call me a pup."

They tossed their T-shirts onto the sand and ran down to the sea. The shallow waters of the bay were warm, but as they swam out to the breakers, the cold ocean currents swirled in and made them gasp. They dived into the rolling surf and came up spluttering and laughing.

"Wow, it's cold," gasped Ryan.

They swam and splashed about until Ryan's teeth chattered and his legs felt numb. "I'm getting out now," he called.

They lay on the sand warming themselves in the sun. "I used to swim a lot with your father," his mother said. "Before he got too busy at work to spare the time," she sighed. "He often said I swam like a seal. He called me his selkie."

"What's a selkie?"

"It's an old Celtic name for seals," she said. "The Celts have an ancient legend about selkies."

"Do you know the legend?"

"Your father's mother, Nana Campbell, told him the selkie story when he was a boy." She looked at Ryan, "Ask him about it sometime." His mother's dark eyes seemed deep and pensive, like the seal pup's, thought Ryan, like a selkie.

"That's what I'll call the pup," he said, "Selkie."

"Copper and Selkie," his mother said. "That's a good choice."

They gathered their things and left the beach under the watchful gaze of the seals.

When school had finished for the summer holidays, Cilla had gone away with her family. Ryan missed her bossy good nature. It was strange not to have her bursting in the door and shouting, "Surf's up, get your wet suit and board," or, "Come on, let's go fishing." He found himself thinking about his friend a lot, and was surprised at how much he missed her.

During the summer, Ryan had visited the seals frequently. At first, Copper was wary. Ryan would go for a swim, then return and stretch out on the sand at a respectful distance. Within days, Copper had accepted his presence and ignored him as he gradually moved closer.

Ryan often watched as Selkie explored the rock pools in the bay. The pup would dip its face in a pool, then shake its head and bleat in surprise. Once it leaned over too far and fell into a pool. It splashed and struggled for a few moments, then rolled and began to play in the shallow water as it discovered its natural element.

Now, as Ryan emerged from the access tunnel, he remembered the hurt look on Cilla's face when he wouldn't let her come with him today. He longed to share the seals with her, but his mother had warned him not to tell anyone else. "Copper and Selkie need to be protected," she had said. "The more people who know that the seals are here, the more at risk they'll be."

At least it would be peaceful at the bay, and he could practise his harmonica. Ryan rounded the point and stopped. A small fishing boat lay drawn up on the sand.

Chapter 2

$\mathcal{A}$cross the bay, Ryan saw a man walking slowly towards the rocks on which Copper and Selkie usually basked in the sun. Today, they were nowhere to be seen.

Ryan jumped onto the sand and began running towards the man, anxious to stop him before he discovered any trace of the seals.

"Hi there," he called.

The man turned around. "Where did you come from?" His face wrinkled in surprise.

Ryan avoided the question. "The fishing's not very good around here," he said.

"I know," the man said. "But I'm curious about a seal and its pup that I saw on the rocks when I sailed past late yesterday. The sea was too high to come in for a look."

"You must have mistaken one of these rocks for a seal."

"There's no mistaking a seal up on its flippers," the man rubbed his bristly chin, "and the pup was a little one, slight, with a small head. It just might be a female, too." He looked at Ryan. "What brings you here?"

"I like a bit of peace and quiet."

The man nodded as if he understood completely. "Ben Kelly's my name," he stuck out a hand. "What's yours?"

"Ryan," he shook Kelly's hand, surprised by the man's hard grip.

Kelly looked over at the rocks, "You haven't seen any seals, have you?"

"I've seen some seal specimens in the maritime museum."

"Lovely coats seals have got," Kelly said. "Nearly their downfall."

"What do you mean?"

"Sealers slaughtered them by the thousands last century." Kelly drew a tobacco pouch and papers from his pocket. He flicked out a paper and spread stringy tobacco along the centre. "The rocks ran red with their blood."

"Why? Why did they kill them?" asked Ryan.

"People liked to wrap themselves up in warm, cosy seal furs." Kelly rolled the paper into a thin tube and licked the gummed edge, then continued,

"And people filled their lamps with the oil from sea elephants." He took a box of matches from his pocket. "A lot of money was made in those days from seals, but a man had to search long and hard for them when I was young." He struck a match, cupped his hands around the flame to guard it from the breeze and guided it to the cigarette in his mouth.

Ryan noticed the man's leather boots with soft fur tops. "Isn't it against the law to kill seals?"

"The last open season was years ago and, apart from a bit of poaching, the seals have been left to breed like rabbits," Kelly said. "But that might all change soon."

"Why should it? What possible harm does a seal do to anyone?"

"It takes a lot of fish to fill a seal's belly. They put a fisherman's livelihood at risk." Kelly drew on his cigarette, "There's talk of a culling season to get their numbers down."

Ryan shuddered. Culling season or killing season, it meant the same thing – slaughter. Ryan avoided glancing at the rocks. Where were the seals? he asked himself. He turned his back on Kelly, "I'm going for a swim."

"A word of warning," said Kelly. "The mother seal must be away feeding, but when she returns don't get between her and the sea. A seal will charge anything that blocks its escape route."

A movement on the shoreline caught Ryan's eye. "Look! Your boat's starting to drift."

"Oh no," muttered Kelly and hurried over the sand. He pulled his boat into the surf and leapt in. The motor sprang to life and he headed out beyond the waves.

Ryan stood on the beach until the boat was out of sight. Then he raced over the rocks, calling, "Copper, Selkie. Where are you?"

As he searched, he tried to imitate the sound he had heard Selkie make when calling to Copper, a warbling ba-aa, like a lamb. He explored all the rocks within the area, calling without response.

If Ben Kelly had seen the seals and found his way into the bay, who else might have been here? Troubled, Ryan sat in the shade of the bushes growing at the foot of the bluff that sheltered the sweep of the bay. He took out his harmonica. Music usually helped to clear his thoughts.

Ryan played a few bars and the notes rang across the bay. He ran his mouth up and down the instrument, blowing hard to clear any obstruction, then played the opening chords of a blues tune. An off-key tremor rose above his music. He lowered the harmonica and listened.

At first Ryan thought the sound was a seagull squawking. Then it seemed to sharpen into a cry. Selkie! It had to be Selkie. He looked around, but there was no movement.

A wail sounded behind him, and he felt the hairs on his neck rise. The bluff formed a solid wall. He turned and parted the bushes, the spiky branches scratching his arms. At the base of the steep bank, a low cave stretched back into darkness.

Ryan bent over and squeezed through the narrow entrance. Inside, the cave opened out into a dome-shaped grotto. After his eyes adjusted to the gloom, he saw a shape against the far wall.

Selkie lay in a dejected huddle. Ryan moved towards the pup, making soothing noises. She raised her head and bleated.

"Take it easy, you're safe now," he murmured and stroked her head. "You've been exploring, haven't you?" After a moment the pup laid her snout on his training shoes.

Ryan sat comforting Selkie, then he gently nudged her towards the mouth of the cave. She baulked at going through the opening, so Ryan went out first and turned to encourage the pup. He could see her snout wrinkle at the smell of fresh air and her whiskers sizing the gap for body width.

Slowly, she emerged into the daylight. The pup's small ears drooped and tears seemed to trickle from the corners of her eyes. She shook herself, snuffled, and headed for the rocks. She scuttled forward, using her front flippers in an awkward windmill-like motion. Waves splashed over the rocks, filling the pools with each swish of the incoming tide.

The pup slid into a pool, revelling in the soothing water. Ryan sat on the edge of the pool, careful not to frighten her. She gazed at him with coal-black eyes. He eased himself into the pool and lowered his face into the water, level with Selkie's black button nose.

As they stared at one another, Ryan sensed a communication between them. Selkie flicked a flipper, splashing him. He imitated the pup by slapping his hand on the surface. Together, they splashed and played in the sun-warmed pool.

A shrill, penetrating cry sounded across the bay. Ryan looked up to see Copper at the water's edge. She stood raised up on her front flippers, snout pointing to the sky. Her wet coat shone and her plump sides showed the success of her feeding trip. Again her sharp call rang out.

Selkie gave a ba-aa in response and struggled out of the water. Copper shook herself and made her way up the beach. Ryan was surprised at the speed of her approach. She moved quickly on all fours, with her back flippers turned forward. He hauled himself from the pool, anxious to put some distance between himself and the mother seal. In his hurry to escape, he slipped on the rocks and scraped his shin and his hand. He scrambled to his feet and ran.

From the safety of the point, he looked back. Selkie was burrowing into Copper's side, guzzling her rich milk.

That night Ryan's mother received a call from a friend who lived near her mother's remote seaside home. She listened intently for a while, frowning. When she replaced the receiver, she turned to her husband, her face serious.

"Mother is very ill, Ian," she said. "She needs me at home."

"Of course," his father said. "Ryan and I can manage for a few days."

"I might very well be away longer than that," she answered.

"Oh?" Ian Campbell sounded wary. He turned his face away from his wife.

Ryan's mother looked at her husband for a long time. Finally, she spoke. "Time apart will be good for us both."

"Take all the time you need," Ryan heard the pain in his father's voice. "Maybe you'll feel happier when you come back."

"I might not want to come back," his mother said very softly.

Ian Campbell turned away quickly, his mouth a hard line. He strode from the room, slamming the door behind him. Anxiety knotted Ryan's chest. He hurried to his room, turned on his stereo, and took out his harmonica. His feet tapped out a rhythm as he began to play, and the music flowed through him, soothing him and blotting out the turmoil in his mind.

In the morning, when his mother hugged Ryan goodbye, he held on to her, wondering when he would see her again. "Look after Copper and Selkie," she said. She reached up and patted his cheek, "And take care of yourself."

The school day passed in a haze, one subject blurring with another. His English teacher noticed his blank page at creative-writing time, "Writer's block?" he said. "You can work on it at home tonight and hand it in tomorrow."

After school, Cilla caught up with him. "Do you want company on the way home?"

"If you can keep up," he said, relieved that she wasn't still annoyed with him.

She poked out her tongue and biked along the road beside him. They stopped at an intersection leading to the coast. "You're quiet," she said.

"My grandmother's ill," Ryan said. "Mum's gone to look after her for a while."

Cilla noticed his strained face and made no further comment. The houses thinned out as they passed through the outskirts of town. They turned on to a side road heading towards the coast. The air became heavy with salt spray. Ryan licked his lips and tasted the sharp tang. The road veered past a sign that read "Ocean Vista No Exit".

Several wooden houses stood among the dunes overlooking a stretch of sand leading to the ocean. They rode past the houses to the end of the road and stopped outside a small cottage. A pathway edged with flowers led to an open door that was painted bright yellow. The house looked very friendly and welcoming.

"It looks like your mother's home," he said.

"Briefly," Cilla made a face. "She's the duty doctor on the late shift at the hospital, so I have to look after my baby brother until Dad comes home."

"Lucky you," said Ryan, laughing at Cilla's scowl. "See you tomorrow."

Ryan walked his bike across the road to his own house, which stood apart, isolated and shaded by trees. He tugged at a loose board by the back door and took out a key.

The quiet house overwhelmed him. He had an urge to yell and shout, to fill the empty shell with sound. Instead, he flopped onto the couch and turned on the television. Cartoon characters flickered across the screen in an hypnotic whirl of colour. He let his eyes close.

It was dark outside when he awoke to the sound of a car door slamming and footsteps on the porch.

"Sorry I'm late." Ian Campbell flung a newspaper parcel on the table. "I stopped off to get fish and chips."

Ryan noticed the grey streaking his dad's flame-red hair as his father bent over to unwrap the food.

"Come on, son. Dive in before the food gets cold."

Ryan pulled out a chair and sat down. He swallowed a piece of lukewarm fish and felt it settle in the pit of his stomach.

"I'll make you some coffee," he said, as his father's head drooped sleepily over the mound of congealing food.

Chapter 3

The following evening Ryan's father came home early with a bundle of papers. He stacked them on the kitchen table and sat hunched forward, making notes and calculations.

Ryan inspected the fridge and found a packet of bacon and some eggs.

"I'll cook," he said. Ian Campbell grunted in reply. Great response, Dad, thought Ryan. He wondered how often his mother had been hurt by the same casual indifference.

Ryan served the meal and sat down opposite his father, who pushed his papers aside and picked up his knife and fork.

"This looks good," he said, smiling.

Ryan remembered the pleasure he had known as a child when his father would come home from work and greet him with a smile. Those had been good days. The house had been filled with laughter, and his parents sat talking for hours in the evening. Sometimes they would all go outside and wait for the first star to appear. "Make a wish," his mother would say when they saw it.

Ryan brewed coffee and waited until his father relaxed back in his chair with the mug cupped in his hands. "Dad, Mum said to ask you about the selkie story that Nana Campbell used to tell you."

His father raised his eyebrows, "I'm surprised your mother remembers the selkies." He drew a deep breath, then gazed out the window at the night sky and began to speak in a faraway voice.

"It is said that one day a year, the seals leave the ocean, shed their skins, and take human form. The selkies, as they're known, then play and sing and dance along the rocky shore.

"One such day a lonely fisherman chanced upon the selkies and fell in love with the most beautiful of them all, a young woman with soft brown eyes and long, flowing hair. He stole her discarded sealskin and hid it in a cave.

"The fisherman crouched behind the rocks and waited. At sundown, he watched the selkies slip into their sealskins one by one and slide into the ocean. All except one, the woman with whom he had fallen in love. As she searched the shore for her skin, he stepped out from hiding. 'Come live with me,' he said. 'Be my wife and I will take good care of you.'

"Unable to return to the sea without her sealskin, the selkie-woman agreed to become the fisherman's wife. Many seasons passed and she gave birth to a son. He grew into a fine lad with soft dark eyes and golden-brown skin. The woman loved her son very much but yearned to return to her own kind."

Ian Campbell lowered his head and gazed into his empty cup for a time. He was silent for so long that Ryan wondered if he had forgotten the story, then he sighed and continued.

"One night the lad dreamt he heard a voice calling him. 'Come down to the ocean, my boy. Come down to the sea.' The boy got up and made his way to a rocky headland. Just before dawn an old seal rose from the waves and spoke to him. 'Look yonder in the cave, my boy. Take what is there and give it to your mother.'

"Rays from the rising sun shone into a nearby cave. Hidden inside, the boy found a bundle tied with fishing line. He unwrapped it and out rolled a silky, golden-brown sealskin. Clutching it to him, he returned home.

"When the lad arrived home his father had already left on a fishing trip. At the sight of her sealskin, his mother wept.

" 'Come with me, my selkie son,' she said. They hurried to the shore, where she slipped into the skin and, turning his face to hers, breathed long and deep into his lungs. Then, taking his hand, she drew him into the ocean with her.

"Deeper and deeper they descended. At first, the boy was alarmed, but he soon found he could breathe beneath the ocean. They passed many wonderful underwater sights, until at last they began to swim upward and finally surfaced in a huge cavern.

"There on a tall rock sat the old seal who had called to him. 'This is my father, your grandfather,' his mother said.

"After several happy days in the seal kingdom, the boy's mother drew him to her. 'You are of human flesh, my selkie son. You must return to the land. But go to the rocks on nights of the full moon. Call to me and I will come.' She wept as they parted, 'Go now with love in your heart for your father, for he was very kind to me in our many years together.' "

Ian Campbell rubbed his forehead in a weary gesture. Outside, Ryan heard the cry of a lone sea bird. His father cleared his throat, then carried on in a tired voice, "The boy's father grieved for the rest of his days over the loss of his beloved wife. The selkie boy grew into a handsome young fisherman with soft, flowing hair and warm brown eyes. Whenever he went fishing, his nets were always filled. And on nights of the full moon, he can still be heard calling from the rocky headland. By and by, a seal will rise from the ocean and talk with him."

They sat in silence, each lost in his own thoughts, until Ian Campbell pushed back his chair.

"Time for bed," he said, then went into his room, closing the door.

A storm lashed the coast in the following days. In the mornings, Ryan and Cilla were blown to school on their bikes and, in the afternoons, they struggled home against gale-force winds. High tides lapped the sand dunes sheltering Ocean Vista and cut off access to the headland. Marine broadcasts warned all craft against going to sea. At least Copper and Selkie will be safe in the bay, thought Ryan.

At first, after all the arguments, it had been almost a relief to live in a silent house. But as the days rolled by, a cloud of dejection settled over Ryan. His father became quieter and more withdrawn. He came home late in the evenings with a pile of paperwork.

Ryan wished he could see his mother and talk with her again. His grandmother refused to have a telephone, "I've got plenty of time to write letters to people with whom I want to keep in touch," she had said.

Twice his mother had walked to a neighbour's place to phone him after he had come home from school. She sounded distant, and their conversation was awkward. After each call, he hung up feeling even more alone.

As the storm dragged on, Ryan paced the house with restless energy. He directed his attention to the untidy kitchen. His mother would hate to see the mess that had accumulated in her absence. He turned the hot-water tap on full, added detergent, and swept cutlery into the sink with a clatter.

He had washed a pile of dishes and was starting to scour the stove when a knock sounded at the door. Without waiting for him to reply, Cilla pushed the door open and entered the kitchen. Ryan tossed her a tea towel.

"You're just in time to help," he said.

"I'm not a slave," she protested. "Mum's off duty, so I came over here to escape my baby brother."

"At least you've got a family," said Ryan.

"Have you heard when your mother's coming back?" Cilla began to dry some of the dishes.

Ryan shook his head. He hadn't told Cilla he had doubts about whether his mother would ever come home. If he said it out loud, it would make it seem real, maybe final. He made cocoa and they stretched out on the carpet in the living room, listening to music. Ryan sipped his cocoa, enjoying the nearness of his friend and the warmth she brought to the house.

The storm eased the next day. When Cilla and Ryan biked home after school, the ocean had subsided to swelling breakers.

"Great surf," Cilla said. "Let's go boarding."

Ryan hesitated. He had hoped to visit the bay to see how the seals had weathered the storm.

Cilla turned her head away from him. "Well, if you don't want to..." she sounded hurt.

"Of course I do," Ryan said hastily. "I'll meet you on the beach in five minutes."

When he pushed open the back door, the house smelled musty and damp. He flung his pack on the table, grabbed a piece of bread to eat, and pulled on his wet suit.

The phone rang, loud and insistent. It was probably his mother. He went to answer it, then changed his mind. Perhaps she would worry about him if he didn't answer. Maybe she would even come home.

Fat chance, he thought. He slammed the door on the jangling of the phone. Taking his board, he raced down the beach and headed into the surf with Cilla. The waves met them head-on. Ryan let them wash over him in a blast of ice-cold clarity. He paddled out to the swelling breakers, turned, then caught a curling, plummeting wave that tossed him onto the shore. Time after time, they challenged the waves.

One powerful wave dumped Cilla into the shallows, rolling her over and throwing her board onto the beach. She scrambled to her feet, water flowing from her glistening wet suit. Her hair clung to her face and rivulets of water trickled down her neck. She's like a selkie, thought Ryan, watching as Cilla pushed her hair back and smiled at him. She retrieved her board and raced back into the ocean.

The wispy clouds were streaked with red from the setting sun when they finally made their way up the beach.

"See you tomorrow," Ryan called to Cilla and trudged through the sand dunes. He dumped his board on the porch and shed his wet suit, ready for a shower.

He had just stepped out of the shower when he heard his father call, "Ryan! Where are you?"

"I'm right here, Dad," he answered. He came out, pulling on his jeans. "You're home pretty early for a change."

"I've bought steak and hash browns for dinner."

At least we'll eat well, thought Ryan. The phone rang again.

"You get it, Dad," he said. "I'll cook."

His father answered the phone. The tired droop of his shoulders lifted as he listened for a moment, then said, "Yes, Ryan's here. We're managing all right." There was another pause before he said, "OK, I'll tell him." He replaced the receiver and turned to Ryan. "Your mother sends you her love."

Ryan flipped the steaks in the pan. "How's Grandma doing?"

"Much the same it seems."

No chance of Mum coming home soon then, thought Ryan.

Chapter 4

On Wednesday morning, Ryan surfaced from a dream in which he was swimming underwater with a shadowy seal shape gliding alongside. A sound had woken him, a voice. He thought he had heard his name spoken. He lay floating in a half-asleep, half-awake state, still cradled in the silky smooth ocean. He heard the voice again.

It was his father making a phone call, "I'll see you soon. 'Bye."

At breakfast, his father said, "I'm going away tomorrow on business." He paused, sounding unsure. "At this stage it's just an overnight trip, and I should be back on Friday evening. But other matters could keep me away over the weekend. I may not be home until Monday evening."

"That's OK with me."

"I'll ask Cilla Hansen's mother if you can stay at their house."

The idea of staying at Cilla's appealed to Ryan, but then he remembered Copper and Selkie. If he stayed at Cilla's, he would never be able to escape to the bay by himself.

"That could be a problem for them," he said. "They haven't got a spare room, so I would be sleeping in the baby's room and he cries a lot. Besides, Mr and Mrs Hansen have enough to do looking after the baby without me underfoot."

"I'm not happy leaving you on your own."

"Dad, you work late most nights and leave me at home by myself," Ryan protested.

"True, but you can always phone me at work if you have a problem," Ian Campbell said defensively.

"How about I promise to phone the Hansens if I need anything while you're away?"

"That sounds fine for overnight," his father conceded. "But I could be away all weekend."

"I can take care of myself for a few days," said Ryan. "I'm not a kid, Dad."

"I don't suppose you are," Ian Campbell looked thoughtfully at his teenage son. "You do seem to have grown up in the past few months."

"Then let me prove I can manage by myself while you're away," said Ryan. "After all, the Hansens are just across the road if I need them."

"I'll give Cilla's mother a call this evening and see what can be arranged," his father said. "I suppose you can't get into too much trouble in a quiet backwater like Ocean Vista."

"Thanks, Dad," said Ryan. "And you don't need to worry about me getting up for school on Monday if you're not home. There are school holidays next week, so I'll just be hanging around here anyway."

Ian Campbell stood up and collected his briefcase. "I'll see you this evening."

When Ryan got home from school, he paused at the kitchen door and studied the quiet room. The house felt empty and lifeless. Throwing his pack on the floor, he sank into a kitchen chair. He couldn't call this place a home any more. It just seemed like a cage in which he ate and slept. Anger flared and Ryan slammed his hands against the table. Flinging back his chair, he went to the sink and splashed cold water on his face. He gasped from the shock and shook his head.

Outside, beyond the sand dunes, the ocean crashed onto the beach. Copper and Selkie came to

Ryan's mind. He wanted to make sure they were all right. He remembered uneasily how Ben Kelly had said that seals were a threat to fishermen.

Ryan went outside and dragged his father's dinghy from the shed. He put in a tin of petrol, his fishing gear, and some bait, then hauled the boat down to the beach. Even though his father had taught him how to handle the boat in rough seas, he had often cautioned Ryan against taking the dinghy out alone.

But Ryan didn't feel up to the long walk over the headland and through the tunnel to the bay. Provided that all went well, he would be back before his father came home, and if he was lucky enough to catch a fish for dinner, perhaps that would appease his father.

Ryan put on a life jacket and pushed the dinghy into the surf. He jumped into the boat and pulled the outboard's starter cord. The motor coughed and died. Ryan tugged on the cord again and this time the engine sprang to life.

He turned the boat away from the beach and steered a course wide of the headland and submerged rocks. Waves crossed the bow and spray cascaded over him.

As the dinghy put-putted past the sheer cliff, Ryan looked across the water at the boulder masking the hidden tunnel. The cliff face looked impenetrable from the sea. On the far side of the cliff, small trees and bushes screened the tunnel exit leading down to the rocky shoreline.

Ahead lay the point and, beyond, the bay. Ryan nosed the boat towards the point and his spirits lifted at the thought of seeing Copper and Selkie again. He skirted the rocks and the bay opened out in front of him. Sheltered by the bluff behind and edged by rocks on either side, the slender curve of sand looked deserted.

He steered the dinghy into the shallows, cut the motor and jumped over the side. He dragged the boat up onto the beach and looked around.

Copper lay on a rock, sunbathing. The pup stretched back over her mother, her stomach exposed and front flippers flopped to either side. Selkie's glossy underbelly glinted in the sun. She lay at peace, her face raised to the sun's warmth. Ryan chuckled as the pup fanned herself with her flippers, which looked ridiculously like wings.

Copper stirred and Ryan drew back. The mother seal wriggled and Selkie moved away from her. Copper then raised herself on her front flippers and waddled over the rocks towards the ocean.

Selkie followed, bleating and yelping. It amazed Ryan how quickly the pup had grown in her few months of life. She now had a firm, compact body with a finely shaped head and inquisitive face. Her jet-black birth coat had moulted and lightened to a silvery grey.

Copper paused and lifted her rear flipper to scratch vigorously behind her neck like a cat. Selkie reached her side and Copper nudged her pup towards the waves surging against the rocks. Selkie whined and raised her soulful eyes in protest. Copper slid into the churning ocean, turned, and swung her head in a beckoning gesture.

The pup drew her body weight back onto her rear flippers, refusing to enter the rough sea. Copper barked sharply and Selkie edged forward. Further and further she leaned, dipping her head into the slapping waves until at last she tumbled in. She struggled for a moment, then her sleek body disappeared under the surface.

Seconds later Selkie's dark, torpedo-shaped head resurfaced. Rolling and gliding, she frolicked in the ocean. She skimmed through the water using her rear flippers to change direction.

Ryan watched her plunge and dive, her hind flippers flicking above the foam like small flags. It surprised him how quickly a creature, so awkward on land, could transform into a graceful mermaid in the sea. No wonder the selkie-woman in the story had longed to return to her ocean home.

A rogue wave thrust Selkie against the rocks and she decided she had had enough. She clambered out and shook herself, spinning out a halo of spray, then flapped over to a warm rock.

Ryan realized with a start that shadows from the bluff had begun to spread over the bay. He needed to leave now if he wanted to return home before his father. He turned around and heard something crunch beneath his feet.

A matchbox lay crushed on the hard sand. Ryan frowned. He remembered Kelly the fisherman using a similar box of matches. Kelly must have come back, but he hadn't harmed the seals. Copper could have been away fishing, and perhaps Selkie had sheltered in the cave again.

Ryan pushed the dinghy into the surf, jumped on board, and started the motor. He steered into the deep water out past the point. Opposite the cliff, he cut the engine, baited a hook, and lowered his line over the side.

Within a few minutes, Ryan felt a sharp tug and his line tightened. He hauled in his catch, a fat blue cod. He whacked the fish on the head and laid it in the bottom of the boat.

Dark clouds began to gather as he pulled on the starter cord. The engine turned over once, hesitated, spluttered, and stopped. He pulled the cord again. The motor gave a half-hearted chug and went quiet.

"Oh no," Ryan muttered. "Now I've flooded the engine."

The dinghy began to drift. Ryan scrabbled in the bottom of the boat, found the two oars and fitted them in the rowlocks. Sculling with one oar, he turned the stern towards the headland. Then he bent forward and dragged back on both oars.

He made slow progress against the strong current and choppy sea. When the heavy clouds let down a splatter of rain, he was soon soaked. His wet T-shirt rubbed under his arms as he rowed.

Dusk had fallen by the time Ryan sighted the lights along the shore. The outline of his house stood in darkness. Relieved, he strained on the oars until he was over the swell of the surf. He hauled the dinghy up the beach and through a small gap in the sand dunes.

Car lights swept into the drive as he stowed the boat in the shed. Fish in hand, he reached the porch at the same time as his father.

"Ryan," Ian Campbell's face was stern. "Have you been out in the dinghy by yourself?"

"I thought you would like fresh fish tonight."

His father opened the door and switched on the kitchen light. "I appreciate that, son, but it's dangerous to go out alone, especially after dark," he said. "Please don't go out alone in the boat again while I'm away."

"OK, Dad," Ryan held up his hand. "OK."

Later, as he washed the dishes and his father dried, Ryan wondered if it would always be just the two of them, like Copper and Selkie. His parents seemed so different, maybe they would never be happy living together again.

"Dad, how did you meet Mum?"

"I was on holiday on the coast when I first saw her. She was up to her neck in the sea, holding on to one end of a flounder net." He paused in the midst of drying a pot, "I thought she was the most beautiful woman I had ever seen, so I swam out to talk to her." He grinned, "The guy on the other end of the net got really mad and roared at me to get out of the way. Then I got tangled up in the net and she ended up hauling me to shore."

"You made a rotten first impression," laughed Ryan. "How did you get over that?"

"She said later I was the biggest fish she had ever caught and she just couldn't bear to throw me back," his father smiled wryly. "I pestered her until she agreed to marry me and we came back here. It was our own slice of paradise, hidden from the rest of the world. We were really happy..." his voice trailed off.

"What happened?"

His father shrugged. "Business has been bad the past year or so. I've had to spend more time at work and take trips away from home," he said. "I suppose your mother got lonely and homesick."

"Maybe it's like the selkie story," said Ryan. "She needed to go back to her own place for a while."

But what if she doesn't come back, he thought. Where would I fit in? I'm her son. Would she leave me here or take me with her? But then I would have to leave Dad – and Cilla.

Ryan sighed. It was too messy, too hard, for him to work out. Anyway, he would have to go along with whatever his parents decided, until he was old enough to take charge of his own life. He put away the dishes while his father phoned Cilla's mother.

Ryan caught snatches of the conversation, then heard his father say, "Well, that's great. Thanks a lot." Ian Campbell replaced the receiver and turned to Ryan. "Mrs Hansen will be home over the weekend. She's happy to keep an eye on you and help if you need anything. She's on call this Sunday, but she says that's usually a quiet day, so she should be around most of the time."

"That's great," said Ryan.

"I'm trusting you to act responsibly, Ryan," his father said. "Don't let me down."

"I won't, Dad."

Biking to school with Cilla on Thursday morning, Ryan recalled his father's farewell. Although he often went away on business, something was different this time. Ryan remembered his father's phone call of the previous day when he thought he had heard his name mentioned. Ryan wondered if there was a connection.

"Your father called yesterday," Cilla said, as if she was reading his mind. "He said he was going away and asked Mum and Dad if they would mind helping if you need anything."

"He seems to think I'll have trouble managing on my own," Ryan said.

"At least he made sure someone is keeping an eye on you."

"I suppose so," said Ryan.

Ryan's attention wandered during morning classes. He thought about his father saying business had been bad. Maybe that was why Dad had been so uptight when he left. It must be pretty rough to see both your marriage and your work fall apart, Ryan thought.

At lunchtime he hurried to the school pool. As he swam, the shadow of his body shimmered along the bottom of the pool. He remembered the shadowy form swimming beside him in his dream and wondered what it would be like to glide through the ocean with Selkie.

Later, Ryan searched for marine mammals in the school library's subject index. A selection of books about the underwater world and its creatures revealed two books on seals. He borrowed both of them.

After the final bell, Cilla joined him on the path leading to the bike rack.

"Dad gave me some money for extra food and stuff," Ryan said. "Do you want to come shopping with me?"

Cilla shook her head. "I have to look after my baby brother again. I think I should change my name to Cinderella."

At the supermarket, Ryan scanned the shelves for a few easy-to-prepare foods. He paid at the checkout, filled his backpack and biked home.

That evening, he lay on the floor in the living room with the books he had borrowed from the library. Legends and folklore surrounded seals. Some cultures believed seals capable of understanding the voice of the ocean waves, believing them to be the link between sea creatures and humans. Ryan read of seals' intelligence and keen sense of hearing.

He hadn't realized there were so many kinds of seals, all with different habits. Some breeds fed their pups for a few weeks before leaving them to fend for themselves, whereas fur seals continued to suckle their mothers' rich, oily milk for months. Although human greed had nearly caused the extinction of fur seals, the pups were also hunted by one of their own kind – spotted leopard seals. It reminded Ryan of the white mice he once had that ate their own young. Even parents couldn't always be trusted, he thought.

The phone rang on Friday morning, as he was getting ready for school.

"Hello, son. Everything all right?" His father's voice sounded remote.

"No problems," Ryan reassured him.

"Good, that's good," his father seemed preoccupied. "I'm sorry, Ryan, but I'll have to stay away for the weekend. Will you be OK until I get back on Monday night?"

"Of course, Dad."

"Phone the Hansens and let them know, all right? Look after yourself. 'Bye."

Ryan hung up, feeling alienated. He shrugged. So what if my father is immersed in his own world? Ryan thought. It leaves me free to do whatever I want for the weekend.

Cilla was unusually quiet as they biked home together after school.

"What's wrong?" Ryan asked.

"I'm going to fail history," she replied. "I'm hopeless at remembering dates."

"Come over when you've finished baby-sitting," Ryan suggested. "We can study together."

"Great. It'll be much quieter at your place," she said and waved as she turned into her drive. "See you later."

Ryan arrived at his house, whistling. He let himself into the silent house. Late afternoon sun shone through the crystal his mother had hung at the kitchen window. Rainbow colours swirled around the room. He cleared away his breakfast dishes and started to get dinner ready. His weekend was off to a good start.

Chapter 5

Ryan felt a bite in the autumn wind as he clambered up the headland on Saturday morning, a foretaste of cooler days ahead. He looked over his shoulder, checking for Cilla. Apart from a dog roaming the sand dunes, the beach appeared deserted.

Hoisting his backpack further up on his shoulders, Ryan continued over the rocks to the sandy inlet overshadowed by the cliff. The access tunnel offered shelter from the wind, but when he emerged on the other side, a sharp gust made him shiver. He slid down the bank and picked his way around the point to the bay.

He smiled when he saw Copper and Selkie playing in the ocean. Copper was floating on her back in a quiet eddy while Selkie nosed up out of the water and launched herself onto her mother. Copper wrapped her flippers around her pup. For several seconds, they drifted together, then Copper rolled over and Selkie tumbled into the water.

Ryan moved towards the seals, eased off his pack, and took out his father's camera. Keeping a cautious distance, he photographed the pair at play. They spiralled, twisted, and dived so swiftly he was unsure whether or not he had captured their graceful, fluid movements.

Tiring of the game, Copper headed towards the shore and hauled herself from the ocean. Snout skyward, she gave the strangled bark that Ryan first heard several months ago, shook herself, and hitched over to the rocks. Selkie flapped after her, yapping. Copper turned to snap at her pup.

Ryan was startled by a dark streak that flashed past and launched itself at Selkie. He recognized the dog he had seen earlier on the sand dunes. It must have picked up his scent and followed him through the tunnel.

The dog sunk its fangs deep into the seal pup's neck. Selkie yelped and whined, shaking her body in an attempt to free herself.

Copper roared and darted her head towards the dog. It edged away, still clinging to Selkie. Copper plunged forward, swinging her head from side to side and slashed the dog on its rump. It howled and released Selkie who let out a *ba-aa* and scurried behind her mother, blood trickling down her neck.

Incensed, the dog turned and sprang at Copper's throat. Ryan picked up a chunk of driftwood and ran towards them.

"Get away, you mongrel!" he shouted, whacking the dog's back. Its grip loosened and Copper shook herself free.

Barking, the dog continued to harry Copper, looking for a way to dart behind her and attack Selkie. It ran back and forth, changing direction swiftly and staying just out of Copper's reach. Then Selkie cried out and Copper turned her head.

In that instant, the dog hurled itself at Copper, clinging to her neck, and biting into the flesh around her ear. Blood spurted from the wound and the seal bellowed. Selkie scuttled for the shelter of the bluff.

Copper reared up, swinging her body. The dog began to slip and clawed at the seal's head, gouging her right eye. In agony, she swayed wildly. The dog slid to the ground in front of her. Copper's head came down and she clamped her jaws around the dog's leg. She shook it, and Ryan heard a snap.

As the dog hobbled away, Copper lumbered after it. She moved with an uneven gait, hampered by the lack of sight in her torn eye.

Powerless to help Copper, Ryan grabbed his pack and made for the bluff in search of Selkie. As he approached the entrance to the cave, he heard the sound of a motor. He turned and scanned the bay, spotting Kelly's boat as it came around the point, waves slapping its sides. Ducking into the cave, Ryan found Selkie huddled against the wall. The pup whimpered as he came near. In the dim light, her eyes were huge dark globes.

Ryan heard the boat chug closer to the shore. He guessed Kelly must have seen Copper by now.

The boat's motor shut off and a roar from Copper sounded a warning to the newcomer. Selkie trembled and whined.

"Quiet now," Ryan whispered. "Kelly must not know we're here." He cradled the pup and stroked her head, avoiding the patch of blood on her neck where the dog had bitten her. Selkie's eyes began to close and her head drooped.

Kelly won't dare go near Copper while she's enraged from her injuries, Ryan thought. He eased the sleeping seal to the cave floor and moved to the entrance. Crouching low, he peered through the scrub shielding the cave.

He could see Kelly's boat riding the shallows and Copper advancing down the sand towards it. Kelly stood up in his boat, holding something in his hand. As Copper reached the water's edge, Ryan realized with a shock that the fisherman held a rifle. Kelly took aim and the crack of a shot reverberated around the bay.

Ryan saw Copper stagger, then turn to run. Another shot rang out and she fell. Behind Ryan, Selkie moaned in her sleep.

Copper lay on the shore, her sides heaving. She lifted her head and it seemed as though she stared right at the cave. Anger churned inside Ryan at the sight of the stricken animal. That coward Kelly! Copper didn't have a chance to defend herself.

The seal struggled to rise, her flippers whacking the sand in distress. She cried out – a harsh, urgent sound. It was the call Ryan had heard the day Copper returned from her fishing trip and summoned her pup.

Selkie stirred and bleated. Ryan rummaged in his backpack and found a sandwich. He placed it in front of the seal and watched Selkie sniff it curiously, then gulp it down.

A guttural howl came from the beach, rose to a squeal, then stopped abruptly. Ryan sprang to the cave entrance. Kelly stood over Copper with a knife in his hand. Ryan watched in horror as the man bent over the dead seal, wielding his knife in long, slicing sweeps. Copper's coat began to fall away from her flesh.

Ryan turned away. Bile rose in his throat and his head spun. He sank to his knees and laid his forehead on the cold rock floor. His breath was rapid and harsh, and his mouth tasted sour.

After a while, he lifted his head and gazed into Selkie's dark eyes. He moved close and gently pressed his nose to hers in the way he had seen Copper do. He felt the pup's breath warm on his cheeks, soft and soothing.

He stayed there for a moment, then sat back on his heels and took a deep breath. He felt drained, but clear-headed. He pulled his pack towards him and took out his father's camera.

Ryan moved cautiously out of the cave and kneeled behind the brush. Kelly had nearly finished skinning the seal. Knife in hand, he stepped back to survey his work. Ryan focused the camera and pressed the shutter button. The *whirr* sounded loud in his ears.

Kelly bent forward to make a final slash, severing Copper's bloodstained pelt from her body. Again, Ryan pressed the shutter. Kelly dragged the seal's skin into the surf. The water turned deep red. Kelly heaved the skin into his boat. He rinsed his knife in the sea, sheathed it at his side, and turned to survey the bay.

Ryan kept still, holding his head low, his heart thudding loudly. He hoped Selkie would keep silent. Then he heard the sputter of the boat's motor. He watched Kelly steer the boat across the waves and disappear around the point.

Silence settled over the bay. Ryan stood up, trying to avoid looking at the abandoned carcass on the shore. He heard a scuffle and glanced down to see Selkie beside him. Snout pointing seaward, she sniffed the air, nostrils flaring, whiskers twitching.

Mewling, she flapped over the sand towards the remains of her mother. Unsure just what to do, Ryan followed.

When he reached the pup she was snuffling over one of Copper's flippers. She nuzzled her mother's side, then raised her head and wailed a thin, high lament. Ryan shivered at the sound, and his own grief rose at the death of Copper.

A chill ocean breeze whipped across the bay, raising the hairs on Ryan's arms and legs. The tide began to creep in and swish around Copper's butchered body. Ryan longed to cover her, to clothe her in her warm sealskin. He remembered the selkie legend and how the fisherman stole the selkie-woman's sealskin, preventing her from returning to the ocean.

Ryan stood in the swirling tide and vowed to find Copper's sealskin and return it to the ocean. The bite of the sea breeze brought tears to his eyes.

"And I'll take care of Selkie," he promised. He put his hand on the pup's head. "Come on, you've got to hide." But Selkie lay down beside her mother in the deepening water. Large grey-brown gulls circled and squawked overhead.

Ryan stood undecided for a moment, then returned to the cave. He collected his backpack and walked back down to the water's edge. He took a sandwich from his pack and held it out to the pup.

At first, Selkie ignored him. Ryan waved the food near her nose, then drew it away again. Selkie turned her head, watching his hand. Ryan dropped the sandwich in the sea. The pup's head darted forward and she swallowed the snack.

Moving back, Ryan produced a packet of crackers. He held one out to Selkie. The pup followed him with her eyes, then slowly moved away from her mother's body and advanced towards Ryan. He rewarded her with a cracker and watched her devour it. Retreating up the beach, he held out another cracker. Gradually, he enticed the seal into the safety of the cave.

Inside, he stroked and soothed the pup, willing her to relax. Selkie stared back at him, alert and watchful. He felt in his pack, but he had exhausted his food supply. His fingers closed around his harmonica. He leaned back against the cave wall and blew softly into the instrument.

Outside, the waves slapped against the rocks. Ryan played a slow, wistful tune he remembered his father humming to him as a child. Closing his eyes, he felt the vibration of the harmonica against his lips and heard the reeds sing. He let the music wash over him.

A long time later, he lowered the harmonica and looked down at Selkie. Her eyes were closed and her body rose and fell in the rhythm of sleep. He took his sweater from his pack and bunched it near her head, then crept from the cave.

Once out of the cave, he sped across the bay, rounded the point, and scrambled up the rocks to the tunnel. He quickly wriggled through to the cliff side and slid over and down the boulder. Breathing heavily he ran across the small inlet and clambered over the headland. Thankful that no one was on the beach to delay him, he hurried over the dunes towards his home.

Inside the kitchen, he flopped into a chair. Thoughts crowded his head. He would have to get Selkie away from the bay. It was too dangerous for her there. Kelly would go back for sure. The fisherman knew Copper had a pup and he wouldn't pass up the chance of another sealskin.

Ryan decided to sleep in the cave with the pup that night. In the morning, he would try to get her to follow him out to sea. The ocean was cold now; he would need his wet suit and his snorkel gear. He rummaged in the fridge and stacked bread, ham, apples, and sardines on the table. He went to the freezer and took out the small fish he kept for bait; he would use them to lure Selkie into the ocean.

The back door swung open and Cilla breezed in. "Hi, Ryan. Mum's invited you to dinner." She stopped and eyed the pile of food. "What's all this for? Are you going away?"

"I was just about to have a snack," he said, feeling his cheeks flush.

"You can't eat all that at once," Cilla said. "You're hiding something."

"Don't be stupid," he said.

"Don't you call me stupid, you red-faced, rotten liar," Cilla accused. "What're you up to?"

"Nothing! Nothing at all!"

Cilla folded her arms. "Tell me your secret or I'll tell Mum you look really sick and she'll rush over here with her medical bag."

"You're a pain," Ryan sighed.

Cilla smiled.

Chapter 6

"And that's everything," Ryan leaned back in his chair. He felt relieved to have told someone about Selkie and the slaughter of Copper. "I'm going back to the bay soon. Thank your mother for the dinner invitation but tell her I can't come because I'm working on a homework project."

"She'll be impressed," laughed Cilla. "I'll say I'm going to help you, then I can meet Selkie."

Ryan shook his head. "There're a couple of things I want you to do."

Cilla frowned, torn between wanting to argue with him and curiosity. "What?"

"I need you to cover for me with your mum. I also need to know where Kelly lives, so that I can get Copper's sealskin and return it to the sea." He picked up a telephone directory and flipped through the pages. "There're a few listings for B. Kelly, but I haven't time to find out which one is Ben Kelly. Will you call and say you're a visitor looking for your fisherman Uncle Ben?"

"Why don't you tell the police about Kelly and let them deal with him?"

"They won't take my word for what's happened," Ryan said. "They would waste time asking questions, and they would probably want to see the bay and what's left of Copper before they even started to find out about Kelly."

"At least you could tell my parents," said Cilla. "They would believe you."

"Even if they did believe me, they would want to call the police. Adults think like that," he said. "Selkie is my responsibility. I have to make sure she's safe before other people get involved."

"I suppose you're right."

"Promise me you won't tell anyone what's happened at the bay."

"All right," Cilla nodded. "I won't tell."

"And will you try to find out where Kelly lives?"

"OK."

"Thanks," said Ryan. He stowed the supplies in his pack and filled a bottle with water.

"What are you going to do when Selkie starts crying for her mother's milk?" asked Cilla.

"She already lasts for days without a drink when Copper goes fishing."

"Maybe she'll manage on what she can find for herself," suggested Cilla.

"She'll have a fair chance of survival if she can catch fish on her own." Ryan said, securing his sleeping bag to his pack with a bungee cord. "Come with me now and I'll show you the tunnel," he said, shouldering his gear. "If you come to the bay early enough tomorrow morning, you can help me get Selkie away."

They climbed over the headland and leapt onto the strip of sand. Ryan showed Cilla the concealed entrance, "On the other side you slide down the bank and go around the point to the bay."

"Take care of yourself – and Selkie," called Cilla as he crawled into the shaft.

When Ryan emerged from the tunnel, full tide had almost engulfed the point. Waves smashed against the foreshore as though the ocean were trying to swallow the land. He jumped from rock to rock between the onrushing waves. His foot slipped on a boulder and his shin scraped down a sharp-edged rock. He waded through knee-deep breakers to the bay and searched the shore.

The beach was deserted. Waves covered the spot where he had last seen Copper; the ocean had claimed her body. Movement near the bluff drew his eye to the scrub. Selkie struggled through the bush and flapped towards the surf, bleating.

Ryan ran across the bay to her. She stopped at his approach, eyes wary, ready for flight. He slowed his pace and moved forward, calling softly.

He took a cracker from his bag and put it on the sand in front of the seal. She swallowed it eagerly, then sniffed his hand, looking for more. Ryan held out his pack and Selkie's snout wrinkled at the fishy smell of the bait inside.

"Follow me," he said and headed for the bluff, trailing the pack behind him. Selkie hesitated, then waddled after him.

An evening chill settled over the bay and mist rolled in from the ocean. Shivering, Ryan entered the cave. His sweater lay on the floor where he had left it. He pulled it on and flapped his arms for warmth. Selkie watched his movements intently. He smiled, perhaps she thought he would sprout flippers.

In the fading light he rationed out some food for himself and Selkie. The seal ate her share quickly.

"That's all you're getting," Ryan said. "We've got to make it last."

He unrolled his sleeping bag, spread it over the cave floor, and slipped into its warmth. Kelly isn't likely to come hunting at night, he thought, taking out his harmonica. Ryan played several fast numbers, the quick pace of his breathing warming him. Selkie lay beside him. She moved closer, propped her head on Ryan's stomach, and slept.

Ryan dozed fitfully, aware of his strange surroundings, the noises of the night, and the strong odour of the seal. Sometime in the early hours he woke to the sound of a night owl's cry. He felt cramped with Selkie leaning against him, so he eased himself from his sleeping bag. He stood up, flexed his legs, and moved quietly out of the cave.

Outside, the mist had cleared and stars sparkled in the night sky. A pale moon cast silhouettes of rocks and brush on the bay. At sea, flickering navigation lights indicated the safe shipping lanes that skirted jagged outcrops.

Ryan saw the shadowy peak of an island rising from the black waters. A brilliant light shone out from the island's hillside to warn ships of the land ahead. The light swung from side to side, sweeping the ocean with its beam. A red beacon shone from the top of the island.

Tomorrow, I'll swim with Selkie out to the island, Ryan thought. He hoped the pup would make its deserted shores her base until she was old enough to search for other seals. Ryan went back to the cave and snuggled into his sleeping bag. Selkie snorted and twitched in her sleep.

Ryan dreamed he was alone in the ocean, struggling to swim to a distant island. Waves swelled up and pushed against him without breaking. Arms flailing, he tried to force his way through the waves, which seemed to be covered with a thick skin. He scanned the sea, looking for Selkie. Where was she? He shouted her name but no sound came. All he could hear was the cry of seagulls circling overhead.

He surfaced from the dream, struggling to free his arms from the tangled sleeping bag. Selkie pressed heavily against him, her body rising and falling like small ocean waves. Relieved, Ryan patted her head and she raised sleepy eyes to gaze at him. She stretched and yawned. Her jaws opened wide to display her bright pink tongue and mouth.

"Phew!" Ryan choked as her fishy breath engulfed him.

Seagulls squawked outside. Ryan stumbled from the cave and watched as the sun began to climb above the horizon. The half-circle of flame shed a path of light across the ocean towards him. He shielded his eyes and looked seaward to the island he had decided to make his target.

"Hey there!" Cilla's voice called to him from the point. She ran across the bay towards him, her hair gleaming in the morning light. As she came near, the anxiety of his dream fell away. It would be all right if there were two of them to help Selkie.

"I brought you breakfast." Cilla put a bag on the sand and took out a package. "Hot dogs," she said, handing him one. "I told my mum we were going to explore around the coast today."

Ryan took a large bite of the warm food. "Thanks," he mumbled through the mouthful.

"One for each of us," said Cilla, clutching a second hot dog.

Drawn by the smell of food, Selkie emerged from the cave. She caught sight of Cilla and froze. Cilla also paused, her hand halfway to her mouth.

"Selkie!" Cilla exclaimed. "She's beautiful." She moved slowly towards the seal.

Uncertain, Selkie began to back away. Cilla made soothing noises as she held out her hot dog.

"Put it on the ground," Ryan said.

Cilla placed her hot dog in front of the seal and moved back a little. Selkie edged forward and began to gulp down the food.

Cilla crept closer and knelt beside Selkie, waiting until the pup finished. Then she extended her hand and Selkie nuzzled her palm. Cilla moved her hand and scratched behind the seal's ear. Selkie tolerated her attention for a moment, then drew her head back.

"I'll get ready to lead her out to the island," Ryan said.

"It's a long way," said Cilla.

"The sooner we get going, the better." Ryan collected his gear from the cave and dragged on his wet suit. Then he picked up his pack with the fish he intended to use to lure Selkie. He strapped the pack to his chest and belted on his fishing knife.

"Time to go," he said.

Ryan carried his flippers, snorkel, and mask in one hand and waved a fish at Selkie with the other. The seal followed him as he moved towards the shore. At the water's edge he rewarded Selkie with the fish and bent over to pull on his flippers.

"Not bad," Cilla nodded approval. "With your wet suit and flippers, Selkie will think you're one of her own kind."

"Try to scare her into the sea," said Ryan. He put on his snorkel and waded into the surf, flapping another fish at Selkie.

"I'll wait for you," Cilla called. She let out an ear-splitting screech, startling Selkie. As Cilla splashed and shouted in the shallows, Selkie scurried forward and launched into the surf, holding her snout up high.

Ryan headed out to sea, feeling the cold water creep into his wet suit. Selkie streaked past him, turned, and dived. Ryan felt a tug on his hand and the fish was gone. Clamping his teeth around the snorkel mouthpiece, he dipped his head below the surface. A dark shape glided beneath him, then doubled back to butt him playfully. Excitement flowed through him. He was swimming with Selkie! He was joining her in her world!

Ryan gave Selkie another fish, then kicked his feet, feeling the flippers propel him forward. He raised his head to sight the island and swam towards it. Occasionally, he would see Selkie's head break the surface as she renewed her oxygen, then she would dive again. After a few minutes, she would reappear some distance from where he had last seen her. She never left him for long. Sometimes he felt her nudge his stomach or chest, searching for more fish.

Treading water for a moment, Ryan looked back to the bay. He waved and Cilla swung her arms in acknowledgment. He felt good knowing she was there. He turned and continued towards the island.

As he swam further out, the sea roughened, slapping against him and tossing him around like a piece of driftwood. A huge wave crashed over him, sweeping him sideways and dislodging his mask. He grabbed at his mask and looked about for Selkie.

She surfaced close to him, rolled over, and with a flick of her rear flippers, she dived again. Moments later the sea boiled and she burst upward, only to sink back under the water as though something dragged at her from the ocean.

In that brief glimpse, Ryan saw her wild-eyed stare and the net around her head. He adjusted his mask and snorkel, loosened his knife from its sheath, and dived. The water churned around Selkie as she struggled to free herself from a discarded fishing net. Her desperate efforts wound the net tighter about her body.

Ryan grabbed the net at the back of Selkie's neck, slid his knife behind the weave, and sliced through the nylon. The net fell away from her head. His snorkel filling with water and his lungs straining, Ryan kicked quickly upward. He surfaced, cleared his snorkel, drew a deep breath, then dived again.

He tugged at the net trapping Selkie's front flippers and hacked at it. One flipper sprang out and he turned to the other, conscious of the tightness in his chest. Within seconds, the net slackened and Selkie twisted free. She flicked her body towards the surface, her rear flippers slapping hard into Ryan's face. He gasped and breathed in water. Thrashing wildly, he clawed upward.

Ryan reached the surface and lay with his chin barely cresting the water, his body limp. Something jolted into him. A nose nudged his face and he stared into Selkie's dark eyes.

He breathed in and choked. Gasping, he drew a shallow breath, aware of a deep ache in his chest. He coughed up brine, the brackish taste scouring his throat. Selkie swam ahead a little, then circled back and butted into him.

"Leave me alone," he croaked. She pushed her snout into his shoulder, then swam forward again, pausing to look back at him.

"OK, OK," Ryan forced his legs to kick and thrust him along in Selkie's wake. The pup was headed back towards the safety of the bay.

Ryan followed her, lifting his arms mechanically and working his legs. He raised his head once and saw the distant figure of Cilla on the beach. A bundle of kelp tangled around his legs. He kicked it away and battled on through the swelling sea. Selkie stayed close to him until they reached the breakers, then she swam ahead. He rode in with the waves until one surged over him, rolled him under, then pitched him into the shallows where he lay gasping.

Ryan felt strong arms encircle him. Cilla tugged him away from the water's edge and propped him into a sitting position. She knelt behind him to support him. Gradually, the pounding in his head eased and his breathing slowed. "Thanks," he said.

"What happened out there?" Cilla asked.

"Selkie got tangled in an old net and nearly drowned both of us." Ryan stood up. "I'm too exhausted to swim to the island now. I'll have to take Selkie in Dad's boat."

"Do you think she'll stay on the island?" asked Cilla. "She came straight back to the bay when she got scared."

"I'll have to get Copper's sealskin to take with us," he answered. "Copper's scent should keep Selkie there."

"I called each B. Kelly in the phone book," said Cilla. "One grumpy guy said he was Ben Kelly and was a fisherman. But he said he didn't have a niece, nor did he want one."

"Where does he live?"

"His address was in the phone book." Cilla took a scrap of paper from her pocket and gave it to Ryan. "97 Seaview Road. That's down the coast road, past where we turn into Ocean Vista."

"Will you stay here with Selkie while I get the sealskin?"

"Of course. I told Mum we would both be away all day."

"There's a tin of sardines among the supplies," Ryan said. "Use them to coax her into the cave. Keep out of sight with her until I come back with the boat."

Ryan went to the cave, peeled off his wet suit, and tugged on dry clothes. He hurried across the bay towards the point, where he turned to wave to Cilla. Selkie was basking on a rock next to his friend, unaware of any danger.

Chapter 7

$\mathcal{B}$ack at home, Ryan loaded petrol and supplies into the boat. He pushed aside a twinge of guilt about taking the dinghy out. He had to get Selkie away from the bay.

He grabbed some bungee cords and wheeled his bike down the drive. He glanced over at Cilla's house and was thankful no one was in sight.

Biking along the coast road, Ryan thought about his failed attempt to help Selkie escape. He was unsure whether his present plan would succeed, but he couldn't abandon her. She had already lost her mother, and he was certain she wouldn't survive without him.

A weather-beaten sign almost hidden by long grass pointed to Seaview Road. No houses were visible from the main road. Ryan hid his bike in a grass-covered ditch and walked down the gravel road leading to the ocean.

Further along, an abandoned cottage stood with its door opening into an empty shell. At the end of the road, Ryan came to the only other house, an old weathered bungalow set back among the trees.

Ryan crouched and moved along the boundary hedge until he came level with an open window. He heard a man speaking and recognized Kelly's voice. From the fisherman's one-way conversation, Ryan guessed he was making a phone call.

"Yeah, it's a good skin, no marks on it. I've got it pegged out in the yard to dry. What's your offer?" There was a pause while Kelly listened. "No way, that's not enough. This season's poor fish catch has left me up to my eyes in debt." Silence again. "Listen, there's a heavy fine for killing a seal. The hide has to be worth the risk I'm taking." Kelly baited another hook. "Look, I'll sweeten the deal. There's also a seal-pup's skin I can get if you name a good price." Kelly waited for a reply. "That's better," he said, sounding pleased with the new deal. "I'll get some more ammunition, then I'll go and search for the pup."

Kelly replaced the receiver and after a few moments a truck's engine whirred and spluttered. The motor revved to a throaty roar, and Ryan saw Kelly drive down the access road in a battered truck.

Ryan made his way to the rear of the house and stopped. Copper's skin was stretched out and tethered to pegs driven into the ground.

Beads of moisture had risen to the surface of the upturned skin, drawn out by the late afternoon sun. Ryan knelt down beside the hide. The strong seal smell filled his nostrils and caught at the back of his throat. He bent forward and worked to free Copper's hide. The skin sagged in the middle as he released one corner. He sat back on his heels and wiped his forehead with his hand.

"You're going back to where you belong," Ryan said, working quickly to free the remainder of Copper's hide. He folded the thick pelt into a bundle and secured it between his shoulders with the bungee cords he had brought from home. It weighed heavily on his back. He hurried along the side of Kelly's house and sprinted down the gravel road to the ditch where he had hidden his bike.

If Kelly sees me, I'm in big trouble, he thought. Head down and legs pumping, he rode along the main road. Sweat trickled between his shoulder blades from the warmth of Copper's pelt. Only a few cars passed him before he reached the Ocean Vista turn-off. With a sigh of relief, he headed towards the beach and coasted home, keeping an eye out for Cilla's parents.

Inside the boat shed, he eased Copper's hide from his shoulders and placed it in the bottom of the dinghy. He took his father's binoculars from a shelf, slung them around his neck, then dragged the boat over the sand to the ocean.

He launched the boat into the surf, riding the waves past the headland and motoring on towards the bay. He felt drowsy as rays from the sinking sun slanted across him. His eyelids closed and he shook himself awake. He couldn't rest until he had Selkie safe on the island.

The boat rounded the point leading into the bay, and Ryan scanned the empty stretch of sand. He beached the dinghy and ran towards the bluff.

"Cilla, I'm back," he called, bending down to the cave entrance.

Scuffling sounded inside, then Cilla's muffled voice answered, "Coming." She scrambled out and stretched. "Selkie makes a great pillow," she said. "Too bad about her body odour though. It really knocks you out."

Ryan grinned as the seal emerged from the cave, blinking in the light. "What a lazy pair," he said.

"While I've been risking life and limb, you two have been napping."

"Did you find Copper's skin?"

"Yeah. But Kelly's going to be looking for Selkie soon."

Cilla watched the seal flap over the sand towards the ocean. "We'll have to get her away from here fast," she said.

"I'll have to get my things together." Ryan entered the cave, filled his backpack, and rolled up his sleeping bag.

Cilla helped him carry his gear down to the dinghy. The receding tide had left the boat stuck in the sand. He pushed it out into the waves. Curious, Selkie joined him in the water and swam between his legs.

"Wait for me," Cilla called.

"Cilla, you can't come," said Ryan.

"But you're always leaving me behind," she protested.

"I need you to cover for me with your parents," he said.

Selkie nudged the backs of Ryan's legs. "Help me get her over the side," he said. "We've got to get her in the first time or she'll take off."

He bent over and stroked Selkie's underbelly. Cilla leaned forward and clasped Ryan's wrists in a cradle under the seal.

"One, two, heave!" They locked their arms, straightened their legs, and catapulted Selkie into the boat. The dinghy rocked violently and the startled seal slid along the bottom.

Ryan scrambled into the dinghy, put on his life jacket, and pulled the starter cord. "Don't tell anyone where I've gone," he said. "I want to find a safe spot for Selkie first."

Ryan steered the boat through the breakers. He turned to look at Cilla standing knee-deep in the water. She raised her hand to wave, and Ryan fought an impulse to turn around and go back.

"Go home now, before Kelly comes," he shouted to her.

Cilla moved back, stopped at the water's edge to wave once more, then sprinted across the sand. She climbed over the rocks around the point and, with a final wave, disappeared from sight.

Ryan shivered as the evening wind tugged at him. He looked at Selkie slumped in the bottom of the boat. Her sides heaved and she raised her dejected eyes to him. He leaned forward and pushed Copper's pelt towards her.

The seal's nostrils flared as the sharp aroma of the hide reached her. She arched her neck and mewled. Struggling forward, she nudged the pelt with her nose. A shudder rippled down her body, and she laid her head on her mother's fur.

Ryan glanced behind at the empty ocean. Good, Kelly hadn't reached the bay yet.

"You're going to be safe now, Selkie," he said. Kelly wouldn't find any signs of the seal when he got to the bay. Then Ryan remembered the dinghy getting stuck in the sand. When he had pushed the boat into the sea, he had left tracks and footprints. It was too late to go back and wipe out his traces. Kelly would know someone had been there.

Ryan didn't want to consider what would happen if Kelly linked him with the seals and the disappearance of the sealskin. If the fisherman remembered Ryan, he hoped Kelly would think he had only gone back to the bay to swim.

Ryan focused on the island. It rose from the ocean like a fortress. The sea darkened to an emerald green as the waters deepened. A shaft of light from the last rays of the sun flecked the underside of a curling wave a lighter green, and the dinghy ploughed on through the swelling ocean.

Chapter 8

*R*yan guided the dinghy towards the island. The rotating navigation light on the hillside swung its beam across the ocean, and Ryan steered the boat past a craggy outcrop at the base of the island. Waves crashed over the rocks in an explosion of white foam.

Further around the island, a gap in the rocks opened out to a small inlet. Ryan manoeuvred the boat into shore and leapt out. He dragged the boat high up on the sand. Reaching into the dinghy he lifted Selkie's head from her mother's hide.

"Come on, girl," he said. "We need to find some shelter."

Ryan hauled out Copper's pelt and leaned on the edge of the boat, tipping it until Selkie rolled towards him. She half-scrambled, half-fell onto the sand. He picked up the sealskin and stumbled up the beach with Selkie waddling behind.

A sweep of light spread out from the hillside and lit up the inlet. Ryan saw an uprooted tree lying above the high-tide line of broken shells. The trunk jutted out at an angle from the base of the hill.

"This will do," he said, spreading Copper's skin in the sheltered V between the bank and the fallen tree. Selkie flopped onto the skin and nuzzled into the fur.

Ryan returned to the dinghy and dug the boat's anchor into the sand. He climbed the rocks shielding the inlet. The navigation light sent a shaft of light across the empty ocean. For tonight, they were safe.

He went to the dinghy, took out his sleeping bag and backpack, and made his way back to the fallen tree. Ryan stretched out beside Selkie, welcoming her warmth in spite of her strong animal smell.

He slept heavily, without dreaming. He woke at dawn, confused, wondering for a moment where he was. Then the memory of Copper's slaughter and his journey to the island flooded back.

Selkie lay sleeping beside him with her flippers tucked under her plump body. She breathed through her nose, and Ryan smiled as her spiky whiskers rose and fell with each breath. He remembered the joy of swimming with her and how she had become transformed from an awkward land creature into a sleek ocean acrobat.

Ryan turned over and looked up at a cheerless sky. It spread overhead like a dome and curved down to merge with the grey ocean. A faint circle of light tried to force its way through the blanket of cloud. Ryan's stomach reminded him that he hadn't eaten for a long time.

He took a sandwich from his backpack and checked his supplies. A few apples, some sandwiches, and a packet of crackers remained, plus a container of water still in the boat. He would survive, but he worried about Selkie. The seal stirred, wrinkled her nose, and bleated.

"Good morning, sleepyhead," said Ryan. He opened the crackers and gave Selkie one. "That's all for now. We need to go fishing for your breakfast."

Ryan made his way down to the beach with Selkie scurrying and snuffling along behind him. His fishing gear was still in the bottom of the dinghy following his hurried arrival home from the bay earlier in the week.

He took his rod and quickly pried a few shellfish off the rocks by the dinghy. He threaded the flesh onto a hook, balanced on a rock, and cast his line into the surf. He soon felt a tug and reeled in, but the fish had escaped.

Ryan baited his hook again and cast his line. This time he caught a small fish, which he unhooked and held out to Selkie. She swallowed it whole, then leaned forward on her front flippers, watching him expectantly. Ryan caught three more fish, which Selkie gulped down, then she pushed her snout into his hand, searching for more.

"Greedy beast," Ryan said.

He felt hot and sticky and stripped off his shirt. He clambered down the rocks and lowered himself into the water. To his delight, the seal joined him.

He lay on his back the way he had seen Copper do, and Selkie glided over to him, placing her snout on his chest. Then she nudged him away and spiralled into the sea. Ryan rolled over and saw Selkie's dark shape twist and turn beneath him. Small fish swam in a school nearby, and Selkie darted among them. She surfaced close to Ryan with her mouth full.

"You sly thing, you knew how to catch fish all along," he laughed. "You can catch your own food from now on."

It pleased Ryan that Selkie was no longer dependent on him for her survival. But she still needed a base on land and that would make her vulnerable when Kelly came hunting for her. At the thought of Kelly, Ryan turned and swam for shore. The dinghy made them easy to spot; he would have to hide it.

On the beach, he pulled the boat behind a curve of rocks and brushed away the trail with a branch from the fallen tree. Although the dinghy was shielded from view, Ryan realized that a quick escape was now impossible. He and Selkie could become trapped in the inlet. He needed to explore the small island for an escape route.

Selkie shook the water from her coat and followed him up the beach. She sat on her mother's pelt, grooming herself. Ryan watched her easily twist her head to reach all around her body. Tired from her fishing trip, she yawned and lay down, closing her eyes.

Ryan took the binoculars from his pack. He looked up at the steep hill and saw twisted tree trunks clinging to the side with corkscrew branches grasping for the sky. A path wound up the hill and he clambered over boulders towards it. He climbed upward, using branches as handholds, and jutting rocks as steps.

The sun came out and shone on Ryan's back, the sweat trickling down between his shoulders. He steadied himself against a bank, removed his shirt, and tied it around his waist. A fly buzzed around him. Irritated, he swiped at it and felt his foot slide. He regained his footing and continued upward.

The roar of the ocean receded as he climbed up the path. His thighs began to ache and his chest felt tight. He cleared his throat to relieve the metallic taste in his mouth. A flock of sparrows rose from a bush in a flutter of wings. Ryan glanced down and saw the inlet far below. The dinghy looked like a toy boat and he could just make out Selkie curled up behind the tree.

The path wound through a patch of bushes. Silence encompassed Ryan, and it seemed as though he had entered a timeless place that hadn't been disturbed for ages. It felt protective, like a sanctuary. Maybe a long time ago it had given shelter to shipwrecked sailors.

The path veered out again to overlook the ocean. Beside the path, the huge navigation light sat motionless against the hill like a sleeping guardian. It must work the same way as a security light, thought Ryan, with sensors that activated the light when dusk fell.

The path narrowed and wound higher and higher. Ryan kept climbing, hugging the hillside. His foot caught on a tree root, throwing him off balance. He stumbled sideways, and the edge crumbled beneath his shoe. Rubble cascaded down and he pulled back against the hill. Not daring to look down, he trudged on.

Finally, the path opened out on an expanse of barren ground at the summit. Dusty soil swirled in the breeze, coating the tufts of wind-burned grass with a fine powder. In the middle of the clearing, a beacon with four red lights encased in mesh sat on top of a wooden pole.

Ryan walked to the far side of the summit and looked down. An almost sheer cliff dropped to the sea. He moved around the edge of the hilltop, searching for an escape route. A landslide blocked one side, and other parts of the hill were covered in dense bushes or jagged boulders. Rabbit burrows pock-marked the occasional grassy hump. The path Ryan had come up seemed to be the only access. The island was both a refuge and a prison.

Wondering if his absence had been detected, he raised his binoculars and looked towards Ocean Vista, focusing on Cilla's house. He felt less alone knowing her place was within sight, although there was no possible way he could attract her attention from this distance.

The windows of his own house looked blank, and Ryan noticed patches of moss growing on the roof. Weeds had regained control of the garden he had worked on with his mother. He thought about how fragmented his family life had become. It was like a sea wall that had been battered by too many waves and had finally crumbled. After talking with his father, Ryan understood the stresses that had caused the damage, but he had no idea if the rift could be mended.

He swung the binoculars over the headland and the deserted bay. Further around the mainland, Ryan spotted Kelly's fishing boat moving along the coast. The fisherman was searching for the seal pup in the wrong place, but it was only a matter of time before he turned his attention to the island.

It worried Ryan that Selkie was easy prey on land. The sea held her greatest prospect of survival. In the ocean she could move out of reach in a flash.

He started down the path. His downhill momentum propelled him speedily along the path, his feet slipping and sliding on the stony soil. He fell once, leapt up, and kept going.

Heart pounding, Ryan reached the base of the hill and jumped over the boulders. He saw Selkie by the tidemark of broken shells, making her way towards the ocean.

"Hey! Wait for me," he called.

Selkie paused and looked back at him, her head tilted to one side. Beyond the breakers, Ryan saw a dark shape dive beneath the water and resurface a few moments later. *That can't be a dolphin,* he thought. *They don't usually swim alone.* He focused the binoculars on the bullet-shaped head skimming the waves.

"It's a seal!" he shouted.

He ran to the boat and put on his wet suit, snorkel, and mask. If he could lead Selkie out to the other seal, it might accept her as a companion. Ryan entered the shallows, with Selkie flapping along beside him. They moved into deeper waters, the cold current seeping into Ryan's wet suit.

Selkie stayed with him until she caught sight of a shoal of fish and snaked after them. He looked around for the other seal and spotted it a short distance away. Selkie's head crested a wave and Ryan beat the water with his hands to attract her attention. She skimmed towards him, happy to join in a new game. Drawn by the activity, the other seal approached them. As it came closer, Ryan thought it looked longer than a fur seal. It moved differently, too. It swayed in a sculling motion. Selkie swam using her front flippers.

Selkie came alongside Ryan and barked a greeting to the advancing seal. With its large, sloping head, it had an almost serpentine appearance. As it plunged towards them, Ryan caught a glimpse of spots glistening on its back.

Ryan positioned his mask to watch the two seals meet underwater. The water churned below him and bubbles disturbed his vision. Then he saw Selkie streak past with the other seal close behind. Horrified, Ryan realized it was attacking Selkie. Of course! The seal had spots, it must be a leopard seal. He had led Selkie to her enemy!

Ryan released the knife at his side. Beneath him, Selkie turned and twisted, rapidly changing direction as she tried to escape. She spiralled up towards Ryan. As the leopard seal closed in, Ryan flicked his knife up. The knife cut into the seal as the predator flashed past, its momentum knocking the knife from his hand.

The leopard seal faltered, its hind flippers thrashing the water as it turned towards Ryan. Blood trickled from a gash in its side as the seal wavered, altered direction, and dived. Numb with shock, Ryan saw it surface further out at sea, then it disappeared from sight.

Beside him, Selkie floundered in distress. A stream of blood spread out from her side where the leopard seal had bitten her. Ryan reached out to Selkie. "Hang in there," he urged. Struggling to keep afloat, he pushed Selkie towards the island.

While in the sea they had drifted, and they now approached a cove further around the island from the inlet. As they neared the shore, a wave swept Selkie away from Ryan and dashed her against the rocks. She collapsed back into the water and began to sink. Struggling to reach her, Ryan saw another swell lift her up and thrust her between the rocks. He reached Selkie and hauled himself up. She lay awkwardly, blood trickling from her side.

"You can't stay here," Ryan said. "You'll get washed back out to sea." Trying to avoid hurting her, he nudged and prodded her forward. Selkie heaved herself over the rocks and flopped down in a patch of weathered grass sheltered by the cove.

Ryan crouched beside her and examined her side. The leopard seal had bitten into Selkie's flesh, but Ryan had intervened before it could do serious injury. He could see the blood already beginning to congeal and the seal's blubber folding around the wound. The pup would need to rest quietly for a while, though.

Ryan looked up at the hillside. From his earlier survey of the island, he guessed the inlet was not that far away. It wouldn't take him long to clamber around the base of the island and bring back their supplies.

Selkie lay with her head stretched out and her eyes half closed. "Stay there, girl," Ryan said as he moved away. The afternoon sun had vanished behind the clouds, and Ryan shivered as he climbed over the rocks. His wet suit clung to his body, hampering his movements. He tried to move as quickly as possible, aware that time was running out for Selkie's escape.

He reached the rocks overlooking the inlet, jumped down, and hurried to the fallen tree. His backpack lay beside the mother-seal's pelt. Ryan stroked the soft fur. "I'm doing my best to look after her, Copper," he said.

He stripped off his wet suit, changed into his clothes, and picked up his backpack containing their meagre supplies. The sea water he had swallowed while helping Selkie had left him with a husky throat and an acrid taste in his mouth. As Ryan knelt by the dinghy to get the water bottle, he heard a boat motor approaching from the direction of the mainland.

"Kelly," he gasped. "It must be Kelly."

Chapter 9

*R*yan glanced around the inlet. It would be useless to hide here. He would soon be discovered. He reached the dinghy and pushed the water container into his pack. He caught sight of a distress flare his father kept in the boat and grabbed it.

The sound of the boat engine drew near. He raced across the sand and scrambled over the rocks towards Selkie. He watched as the boat skirted the outcrop and approached the inlet.

Kelly stood at the wheel of the boat, guiding it towards the shore. The fisherman cut the motor and it spluttered and died. Ryan's ears ached in the silence that followed, and he swallowed to ease a tickle at the back of his throat. It would only be a matter of minutes before Kelly found his boat and began searching for the owner.

Ryan looked up at the hill. The only way out was to climb, and even then there was no escape. At least it would buy some time, he thought. He shouldered his pack and leapt over the boulders towards the path winding up to the summit.

He clambered up the hillside, grabbing at branches for support. As he hauled himself up and over the thick roots of an ancient tree, he glanced down at the inlet.

Kelly was standing beside the fallen tree, looking at Copper's pelt. Ryan realized the fisherman would guess that whoever was on the island also knew he had slaughtered the seal. Kelly gazed across the sand at Ryan's footprints leading to the rocks. He moved to follow the tracks.

If he keeps going around the base of the island he'll find Selkie's cove! thought Ryan. He had to draw Kelly away. He picked up a rock and heaved it. It bounced off the side of the hill, dislodging a clod of earth and small stones, which clattered down the hillside.

Kelly looked up and Ryan allowed him to catch a glimpse of his face before he pulled back. He heard the fisherman's boots scrape on the rocks at the bottom of the hill. Kelly was coming after him.

Ryan slipped out from behind the tree and entered the sheltered patch of bush along the path. He had no idea what to do next, except a conviction that he must lead Kelly away from Selkie. He kept climbing, his heart thudding and his throat burning.

The path wound outward and brought him alongside the navigation light. Ryan stopped and stared at it. It would soon be dusk, and the light would sweep the island and its waters, making it easier for Kelly to spot Selkie.

Ryan found a sturdy branch and swung at the thick glass protecting the light. A small crack spread across the curved shield. He swung again and a shower of glass exploded from the light. A bulb sat in the middle surrounded by a reflector. He rammed the end of the branch into the bulb, shattering it.

Ryan heard some branches crack below him and guessed Kelly had made it nearly halfway up the hill. That gave Ryan a good lead. He hastened up the narrowing path towards the hilltop, pushing his aching legs onward.

He staggered into the summit clearing and dropped to his knees, gasping for breath. He slid off his pack, pulled out the water container and took a long swig. Water trickled from the edges of his mouth and down his neck.

Ryan took the binoculars from the pack and climbed to his feet. The Ocean Vista houses stood out like a haven. He saw a plume of smoke rise from the chimney of Cilla's house. Cilla must be home by now! He grabbed the distress-flare container from his pack, pulled off the cap, and shook out the flare. Holding it upright, Ryan released the safety pin and flicked off the cap.

The flare ignited and rocketed upward, flame shooting from the end. It soared high into the sky before a small parachute opened and a cloud of red smoke billowed out. He thought Cilla probably wouldn't see it, but it was his only hope. Time seemed to stop while the parachute hovered over the island, then it faltered and fell, trailing its fading signal.

He heard Kelly approach the summit and turned to face him. The fisherman stumbled into the clearing. Recognition flickered as he glared at Ryan. "You're playing a dangerous game, son."

"What do you mean?"

"Don't mess me about! Did you really think you would get away with stealing my sealskin so you could make some easy pocket money?"

Ryan's thoughts raced. He was surprised by Kelly's accusation that he had taken Copper's skin to sell for himself, but it gave him a chance to gain more time for Selkie.

Kelly stood watching Ryan intently. "You know where the seal pup is, too, don't you?"

"She's gone," said Ryan. "Out to sea."

"Don't lie to me," Kelly moved closer and gripped Ryan's arm. "Take me to her. Now!"

Ryan looked defiantly at the older man. "What's in it for me if I show you where to find the pup?"

Kelly stroked his chin. "Fifty bucks."

Ryan shook his head. "Eighty."

"You're hardly in a position to bargain," Kelly said. "Sixty dollars, and that's final."

Ryan nodded agreement.

"Let's get a move on then," said Kelly. "It'll be dark soon."

Ryan bent to pick up his pack and Kelly trod on his hand. "Leave it," he said.

"There's food in there for the seal," said Ryan, flexing his crushed fingers. "It will make it easier for us to get near her."

"OK, pick it up," said Kelly. "Let's go."

On the way down the hill, Ryan considered ways of escape, although he knew it was unlikely he could shake off the fisherman. Even if he did manage to get away from him, where could he go? The only exit was by sea. And Ryan knew he wouldn't last very long in the ocean without his wet suit.

Near the bottom of the hill a rabbit darted out from a clump of grass and shot across the path in front of Kelly. The fisherman stumbled and Ryan sprang forward.

"No you don't," Kelly grabbed Ryan's pack. Ryan felt himself dragged backward.

"Don't give me any trouble, got it?" said Kelly, grabbing his arm. He held on to Ryan until they reached the bottom of the path, then he shoved him over the boulders.

"Get that sealskin and put it in my boat," he ordered.

Fighting back his anger, Ryan picked up Copper's pelt and carried it down the beach. Kelly reached into his boat and took out his rifle.

"You can't shoot her," said Ryan. "She's holed up in a cove under a cliff. A rifle shot could ricochet back on us."

"Then I'll have to club her, just like the old sealers," said Kelly, picking up a strong branch with a gnarled end. He stowed the rifle back in the boat and took out a large torch, which he shone right in Ryan's face. "Well, where do we go?"

Ryan turned away from the light, feeling sick with defeat. Kelly had already sailed around the mainland side of the inlet and would know the seal was not in that direction. There was no other option but to take him over the rocks to the cove.

"This way," he said.

A biting wind whipped foam into the air, and evening clouds darkened the ocean. Ryan stumbled over the rocks, taking as long as he possibly could. Kelly followed him, the light from his torch dancing across shallow pools and sending crabs scuttling for cover.

When they reached the cove, Ryan turned to Kelly. He had a desperate urge to try and overpower him. But he knew that one blow from the heavy club the fisherman carried would knock him senseless. "We're here," Ryan said.

Kelly shone his torch into the dark recesses of the cove. The beam travelled over a dark hump pressed against a rock. Ryan's heart ached at the sight of Selkie cowering from the light. The only thing he could do for her now was to stall Kelly.

"I'll draw her out from the cliff," Ryan said. He moved towards Selkie and knelt down beside her. "There, girl," he said, stroking her head. "Take it easy now."

He took off his pack and found a sandwich. He offered it to Selkie, the stale bread crumbling in his fingers. The seal gulped it down and snuffled into his hand searching for more food. He could see that her side had begun to heal. It was so unjust that she had survived attack from her natural enemy only to be trapped by a thug like Kelly.

The fisherman edged forward. "Bring her out a bit further so that I can get a clear swing at her," he said, gripping the club. Selkie tossed her head and barked as he moved near.

Ryan stood up and faced Kelly. "Do your own dirty work," he said.

"What's the matter?" sneered Kelly. "Haven't got the stomach for it?" He stepped forward, weighing the club in his hand.

Above the sound of the surf breaking on the rocks, Ryan heard the high whine of another boat.

Kelly turned off the torch. "Get back out of sight," he said. "And don't make a sound." Ryan felt the sharp point of a knife jab into his side.

A shore patrol boat rounded the island, its powerful searchlight probing the waters and shoreline. The beam passed over the rocks and swung towards the cove. Kelly moved back, stumbling over Selkie. She snarled, reared up, and lunged at him, her teeth slashing into his thigh. Kelly dropped his knife and yelled.

"What's going on there?" demanded the captain, aiming the searchlight into the cove.

Selkie hung on to Kelly, shaking her head back and forth like a dog with a rabbit. The fisherman struck her on the head and pulled free. Howling with pain and rage, he splashed through the water towards the patrol boat.

"You're just in time," he called. "I saw this kid in the cove while I was out fishing. I beached my boat and climbed around to see what he was up to." He pointed a finger at Ryan, "The little beast pulled a knife on me."

"Don't believe him," shouted Ryan. "He was going to slaughter this seal."

"The kid's just trying to save his own hide," said Kelly, climbing into the patrol boat. "I got here just in time to stop him killing the pup."

"He's lying!" shouted Ryan.

"Come on, lad," called the captain. "You'll have to come back with us so we can sort this out."

Ryan dropped to his knees and put his arms around Selkie. "At least you're safe," he said. He had kept his promise to Copper. "Look in his boat at the inlet!" he shouted. "He's got a sealskin in it." Ryan grabbed his pack and pulled out his father's camera. "And I can prove how he got it," he yelled, wading through the water to the patrol boat. "I've got photos of him slaughtering the seal and skinning her." One of the crew leaned over and helped Ryan climb into the boat. Kelly glared at him.

"Did you see my distress flare?" Ryan asked the captain. "Is that what made you come?"

"We received a report of a flare in this area," the captain answered. "We noticed the navigation light was out and thought something must be happening on the island."

The patrol boat motored into the inlet. Another member of the crew went over to Kelly's boat and shone a torch in the bottom. "The lad's right," he said. "There's a sealskin here."

The captain turned to Kelly. "We're confiscating your boat," he said. A tow rope was tied to the bow of the fishing boat.

"Can I follow you in my father's dinghy?" Ryan asked the captain.

He nodded and Ryan waded ashore. He pushed the dinghy towards the surf and climbed on board. The patrol boat skirted the island, with Kelly's boat trailing behind it.

Ryan followed, relieved to be going home. A deep tiredness settled over him. His every action seemed to happen without thought or feeling, as though he was on autopilot. He longed to lie down in a warm bed and sleep.

Chapter 10

The lights of Ocean Vista flickered through the mist as the patrol boat towed Kelly's boat towards the jetty. Several officers helped dock both boats and took custody of Kelly.

Ryan coasted into the jetty and flung a rope to a man who caught it and tied it around a bollard. The man bent down and held out a hand. Looking up, Ryan was surprised to see it was his father.

"I'm so relieved that you're all right, son," Ian Campbell said.

Ryan took his father's hand. He climbed onto the jetty and felt it shake beneath him as footsteps pounded along the boards. Cilla burst out of the mist and flung herself at Ryan. He reeled back against the bollard, feeling her arms encircle him. She made a sound like a sob mixed with a chuckle. "You smell awful," she said.

He laughed and held her away from him. "Same old Cilla," he grinned. "Was it you who saw my distress flare?"

"No, it was Dad. He had just come home when he saw the flare. I heard him phone the shore patrol and I realized you must be in trouble," Cilla faltered. "I had to tell my dad about Kelly and the seals. He called the police and we've all been waiting, hoping the patrol boat would find you."

"It's OK. Help came just in time," said Ryan.

"When I found you and the boat gone I was worried," Ian Campbell said. "I went to the

Hansen's, and Cilla told me what's been happening." He put his arm around Ryan's shoulders, "You've been very brave, son, but you took an awful risk."

"I had to, Dad," Ryan said. "Selkie really needed my help."

"Is she safe?" asked Cilla.

"I think so," said Ryan.

An officer approached Ryan. "We'll need a statement from you," he said.

"He needs warm clothes and food first," Ian Campbell said. "Can you talk to him at home, in an hour?" The policeman nodded in agreement.

Cilla tugged at his arm. "Come on," she said.

As they walked home, his father said, "Your mother phoned earlier and I told her what little I knew. She was very upset."

"I didn't mean to cause so much trouble, Dad."

"I know you wanted to protect the seal, but you shouldn't have taken the boat out on your own again," his father said. "But I suppose we've both made some mistakes. I haven't been totally honest with you, either."

Ryan stared at his father in amazement. "What do you mean?"

"Business took me to the area where your grandma lives," he replied. "I arranged to see your mother. I didn't tell you because I didn't want to get your hopes up if nothing came of the visit."

That explained why he was so tense about going away, thought Ryan. "How is Mum?"

"She's fine," his father said. "We talked a lot. I'll tell you about it later."

At home, Ryan stood under the shower for a long time, letting the water flow over him. His skin tingled as warmth slowly returned to his body. The phone rang as he was dressing. He heard his father speak for a moment, then call up to him, "Ryan, it's your mother."

In the kitchen, Cilla and his father were busy preparing a meal. Ryan picked up the phone, "Hello? Mum?"

"Ryan! Are you all right?"

His mother's voice sounded so full of concern, Ryan found it difficult to speak at first. He longed to see her again. "I'm fine, Mum," he finally managed to reply.

"That's a relief," she said. "Ryan, no matter what has happened we can work it out."

"It's a long story."

"Don't worry about it just now. You sound very tired," she said. "I'll come home tomorrow and we can talk then."

"That'll be great," he said. He wanted to ask if that meant she was coming home to stay but he didn't know if he could cope with the answer right now. "How is Grandma?"

"She's well enough now to manage with some help from her neighbour."

"That's good," said Ryan.

"I'll see you tomorrow," his mother said. "I love you, Ryan."

"I love you, too," answered Ryan, and he replaced the receiver.

Cilla put a plate piled with food in front of him and sat on the opposite side of the table with a cup of cocoa. Two officers came and, in between bites, Ryan told them about the slaughter of Copper and subsequent events.

As the warmth of the kitchen and the food sank in, a deep weariness enveloped him. His own voice sounded distant and his words slurred.

The policemen stood up. "That's enough for tonight," said one. "When Kelly appears in court, you'll have to repeat your story for the judge."

Ryan remembered Copper's pelt. "Can I have the sealskin back?" he asked. "I promised to return it to the sea."

"We'll need it as evidence," said the officer. "But the judge will consider your request."

Ryan woke to daylight streaming through the bedroom window. He remembered his mother was coming home today and climbed out of bed. First, he had to find out if Selkie was all right.

He heard the back door open and Cilla's voice call out, "Anyone home?"

"Come on in," his father answered.

Ryan quickly pulled on his clothes and went into the kitchen. Cilla and his father were sitting at the table.

"Why aren't you at work today, Dad?" he asked.

"I thought I'd better clean up this place before your mother comes home," his father said.

Ryan sat down opposite his father. "Dad, there's something I need to do."

"What's that, son?"

"I need to check on Selkie," Ryan answered. "Please, can I take the dinghy to the island?"

His father looked doubtful. "I'm not sure that's a good idea."

"I'll go with him this time," said Cilla. "And I won't let him do anything stupid."

Ryan frowned at her bossy tone, but his father laughed. "I'm inclined to believe you, Cilla," he said. He looked at Ryan, realizing how important it was for him to know the seal was safe and well. "Very well, but you're to be back before your mother arrives this afternoon. She'll be anxious to see you."

"Thanks, Dad," Ryan sighed with relief. "I'll be careful."

Cilla helped Ryan pack food for Selkie, and together they launched the boat. Ryan became anxious as they approached the island. After all he and Selkie had been through, he was fearful for her. She was still very young and quite vulnerable to predators, both on land and in the sea.

They cruised past the inlet where he and Selkie had sheltered and motored around the base of the island. Ryan leaned forward as the cove came into view. Beach grass swayed in the breeze and waves lapped the empty shore.

"Selkie!" Ryan called. "Selkie! Where are you?"

"She's not there," said Cilla.

"She's got to be here somewhere," Ryan edged the boat in closer. "She can't have left!" He scanned every nook and crevice in the cove. "She can't survive on her own."

"Are you sure?" asked Cilla.

"Of course, I'm sure," he replied. "She needs me. I've got to find her." He pushed the throttle forward. The engine revved and the boat spun around, spraying out a foaming jet. Cilla hung onto the rail and bit her lip.

Ryan gunned the boat forward, and sped beyond the shelter of the island. He gripped the wheel and his body strained forward, eyes searching the ocean ahead.

Cilla saw it first. "Over there," she pointed. "What's that?"

Ryan slowed the boat and edged towards the dark shape. "It's a seal!" he said.

As they came closer the seal dived. Ryan stood silent, waiting for it to resurface.

"Was it her?" asked Cilla. "Was it Selkie?"

"I don't know," he answered. His voice sounded flat, drained of all emotion.

Bubbles rose beside the boat and a seal's head burst from the water. It looked at them, then glided a short distance away and rested on the surface.

"My pack!" Ryan rummaged in his pack and took out his harmonica. He drew the instrument across his mouth, blowing into the reeds. The music floated across the ocean. The seal turned her head, yelped, and swam towards the boat.

When she reached the side, Ryan knelt down and stretched out his hand. The seal nosed into his palm. "Selkie," he whispered and stroked her head. The seal raised her dark eyes and looked into his.

A series of high-pitched calls sounded in the distance, like seagulls circling a shoal of fish.

"Look," said Cilla. She pointed to where a group of fur seals leapt and dived in the waves.

Selkie turned her head and spiralled into the water. They saw her surface further out. Again the seals called their high, yelping greeting. Selkie barked in reply and swam towards them.

Ryan watched as the seals spread out around her, then enclosed her in their midst and moved away. He strained to see as the dark shapes became small dots and disappeared from sight.

Cilla touched him gently on the arm. "It's time for us to leave."

Ryan stood gazing out to sea for a moment longer, then he started the engine and turned the boat towards the mainland. He looked sideways at Cilla.

"You know," he said, "there's an old story my grandmother used to tell about the seals..."

Appendix – Selkie Spellings

The Celtic legend of the selkie comes to us from a long tradition of oral storytelling. When people began to write down the story, they used many different spellings for the word "selkie", depending on the dialect of the storyteller. Following are some of the other spellings:

silkie   *selchie*
selky   *silky*

From the Author

The seeds for *Call of the Selkie* were sown when I read the selkie legend to my youngest son, Tony. Seals are intelligent creatures, and some ancient cultures believed they were the link between sea and land. I hope readers of *Call of the Selkie* will gain an appreciation of fur seals and the special relationship that can exist between humans and animals.

I would like to extend special thanks to Bruce Dix for offering me advice and sharing his expert knowledge of fur seals. I would also like to thank my husband, Owen, for his support, and writers Sherryl Jordan and Phyllis Johnston for their friendship and encouragement.

Jean Bennett

From the Illustrator

I was born in Colorado, and have been drawing since I was three. I live with my lovely daughter and scuba buddy, Nicolle, and my son and favourite baseball pal, Paul.

I would like to thank Matt Anderson and Stephanie Walker for modelling for the illustrations in this book, and Megan and Rebecca Anderson for their help with setting up the photographs on which the illustrations are based.

I would like to dedicate this book to Daniel Shea, who gave me art, and Elaine Shea, who gave me faith.

Shawn Shea

That's a Laugh

Thrills and Spills

Challenges and Choices

Our Wild World

© Text by **Jean Bennett**
© Illustrations by **Shawn Shea**
Edited by **David Nuss**
Designed by **Gary Haney**

© 1999 Shortland Publications

09 08 07
10 9 8 7 6

Published in Australia and New Zealand by MIMOSA/McGraw-Hill,
8 Yarra Street, Hawthorn, Victoria 3122, Australia.
Published in the United Kingdom by Kingscourt/McGraw-Hill,
Shoppenhangers Road, Maidenhead, Berkshire SL6 2QL

Printed in China through Colorcraft Ltd., Hong Kong
ISBN 10: 1-57257-737-1
ISBN 13: 978-1-57257-737-4